I0816421

Don't Forget to Love Me

Don't Forget to

Wave Books
Seattle/New York

Anselm Berrigan

Love Me

Published by Wave Books
www.wavepoetry.com

Wave Books titles are distributed to the trade by
Consortium Book Sales and Distribution
Phone: 800-283-3572 / SAN 631-760X
Library of Congress Cataloging-in-Publication Data
Names: Berrigan, Anselm, author.
Title: Don't forget to love me / Anselm Berrigan.
Other titles: Do not forget to love me
Description: First Edition. | Seattle : Wave Books, 2024.
Identifiers: LCCN 2024008732 | ISBN 9798891060081 (paperback)
Subjects: LCGFT: Poetry.
Classification: LCC PS3602.E7635 D66 2024 | DDC 811/.6—dc23/eng/20240226
LC record available at https://lccn.loc.gov/2024008732
Designed by Crisis
Printed in the United States of America
9 8 7 6 5 4 3 2
Wave Books 117

THEORIES OF INFLUENCE

Wobble Factory

JOHN COLETTI IMITATION RACKET

Big Sketchbook Semi-Survival Poems

lean towards gimmick —Claire Hong

epigraphic
 epigrammaphone
 epitaffy (salt water)
 epigraphite

THEORIES OF INFLUENCE

In Betweener

The sun got its new angel wings tee-shirt
smudged with the sandbox's finest
demi-mud. This would render
appearances partial, with a cornball's
incongruence. Sidewalk chalk radioactive
Well, we'll never write that letter to
the lozenges, I mean that shrinking
postcard on the way to Saturn
Will someone please hand me
my martini, so I can
make it through this
The   awful ordeal?
title   Name there
placed   in the palm
the   of your natural
action   tremor
off-center
rendering that floating
green eye, well
it floated

off onto some

bell somewhere

Yesterday's duck

seemed to have three parents: a vulture

a turkey, & a something

a plastic

shapeliness

unaccountably

signaling Dark Star

Winged creatures

suspend shyness

& we were stabbed

with permission

all over

& again, the assemblages

of guilt

frozen in dispossession

Did that closet just murmur?

“No mere solar beam can harm the lord of photosynthesis”

“No barrier can stop one who dwells between all boundaries”

“Welcome back to life, my former foes”

“& be tied to the end of your string / flying in the air babes at night”

Press Conference

Do you really believe stability is stable
Imitating copied weight by copping a plea

I'm just here so I don't get fined
We did do a good job of executing

Imitating copied weight by copping a plea
I'm completely out of curvaceous toucan

We did do a good job of executing
I never noticed your nonchalant decay

I'm completely out of curvaceous toucan
Prone to milking figs & bilking fig newtons

I never noticed your nonchalant decay
But I was born sliding out of the plane

Prone to milking figs & bilking fig newtons
Photographs copy me too personally in nature

But I was born sliding out of the plane
Chilling like a villain on a Grecian urn

Photographs copy me too personally in nature
Do you really believe stability is stable

Chilling like a villain on a Grecian urn
I'm just here so I don't get fined

for Marshawn Lynch & John Yau

Binge Better

The local sign commands
Stick this somewhere

And take a picture
Of the way

All its parts
Refuse to come

Together other
Than as equal

Units of color.
The next show

Begets its funky
Irradiated quality

Shepherd style
By the roadside

Shadow produced
By an old bus's

Moving lean. I am
On that bus, flirting

With red clay
Ditch & Savannah

Dust. Zebras bolting
From the side

Of the road
In triplets

Constitute a wave
Of presence in key

With a row of pigeons
Taking it easy

On the line
where sky meets

utility. The next stop
is Beverley Road.

for Christopher Okemwa

*****

I would like to have a pounce of pigeons
I would like to have a door of dark matter
I would like to have a fleece of indignity
I would like to have a solitude of phrases
I would like to have a gutter of daisies
I would like to have a jackknife of tugboats
I would like to have a screen of chemistry sets
I would like to have a goldfish of ashtrays

The Other Shoe Issue

I'm not crazy about the way
these glasses make me see
agh, June threw her shoe
her red sneaker of the left
foot into this mailbox
disguised as a garbage can
designed to keep rats
like me from entry &
the green cap which wields
person with key cannot
be found though we scans
the park's perimeter
looking for it and her
& the possibility of re-
solving the shoe issue
she is standing on
a swinging tire with
Lorca, June that is
this is the clearest
thing that's happened
to me in ages, epochs
& eras in semi-fact
replacement shoes are
arriving imminently
given I'm carrying them
back from home already
who knows what else
might be in the can
with under and in the
little red sized shoe

or who, no shark
wants to eat you
but one might be
hungry when you're
nearby in that wetsuit
I've never directly met
anyone either mister page

*****

She's feeding the local birds
Bemoaning upstaters who
Let their dogs off the leash
In the park—today this park
Is finally not crowded enough
For me to have to pass through
Without sitting on one of its
Gnarly comfort benches
The crank degeneration
My last secret freind
Friend; I forget how
To spell freind/friend
Fried N, ok, friend
Chalk hearts are cheesy
But not when saccaded
Through by pigeons &
Hopped through by
Sparrows getting to
Know you. The blue
Jays, warblers, robins
Red-tailed hawks &
Grackles & woodpeckers
Remain reticent, rightly
Regarding CONTACT.
The Starlings tho
Signal conversation's
Possible later, maybe.

yes , I knew that I always would

certain shopping carts

may contain fire escapes

*****

"Of the societal construct that is dinosaurs" —from a fantasy basketball text thread

*****

talk about a thing
with great separation
between definition
& understanding

(finger
rolling
in space
next
to ear)

Theories of Influence

I do not know how I got through the first
day after the storm but recall that during

the night, doubting what I had seen
with my own eyes I walked once more

through the park. Where and in what
time I truly was that day in Orfordness

I cannot say even now as I type these
words. I cannot say how long I stood

by one of the three windows, engrossed
in that view. Whenever I rested on that bed

over the next few days, my consciousness
began to dissolve at the edges, so that at

times I could hardly have said how I
had got there or indeed where I was.

I have only an indistinct notion of how
beautiful it all was, said Anne, nor can I

properly describe now the feeling of being
driven in that limousine that appeared

to have no one at the wheel. I cannot
remember whether it was she who

turned the conversation to the fact
that nobody wears mourning any more

not even a black band on the sleeve
or a black stud in the lapel. But why

it was that on my first visit to Michael's
house I instantly felt as if I lived or had

once lived there, in every respect precisely
as he does, I cannot say. Instead I left

the building with a sick feeling in the pit
of my stomach & walked & walked without

being able to grasp even the simplest thought
well past the Westkreuz or the Hallesches

Tor or the Tiergarten; I can no longer say
where. I cannot say how long I walked about

in that state of mind or how I found a way
out. I no longer remember if it was the Lord

Asquith the Aristo or the Fabiola. To this day
I do not know what to make of such stories.

after W. G. Sebald

Proof ("everything you are gone slightly mad . . .")

. . . find a way of living with the illustration that Johns breaks down
into formal elements & scuffs up with paint . . . —Marjorie Welish

biking east by the former Boys Brotherhood Republic sign on 6th between
avenue D and the FDR, I remember the facade of that brick brown building
being the last ever place leaning in I saw my father & wonder can I prove it?
Curious commissioned question covering for the intensity of a repeated feeling
jacking out from a defunct sign who asks where you are all the time
intention loves the back seat, the bent interstices & karnal bunts of who's looking
will be the deciders of a little, my name misspelled in Free Cell, caveat
of an early-aughts underground, I'm 47, my daughters 8 & 11, I don't have
no I do have a ticket stub for Nelson Mandela's powerful measured speaking
at Yankee Stadium in 1990, I never *really* think, I say at times, to myself, the cat's three
surgeries cost as much as one or two of my three adjunct jobs generally pay per semester, I
forget which ones, when I wrote, privately, one cannot control an army of imaginations, I
believed I was referring to protestors in 2011 in Tahrir Square, I was 10 & my brother 8,
almost 11 & 9, when our father, close to 49, died in 1983, I live four blocks & one avenue
away from the apartment we lived & he died in

I demand change from myself in writing & not in living I am told, I voted
for Nader in 2000 to raise money for the Green Party, knew New York
would go Gore, I'm really typing this in order to get go gore into the poem
coming out of proofs I had two expired driver's licenses from one Rick Pytlik
in Buffalo before I turned 21 the bouncer at The Continental mystistymied &
amused let me in but I do not know English because I didn't respond when
a stranger told me not to look so serious the day after my sister Kate
was killed on Houston Street by a motorcycle & its driver, four years
after her arrest in the crown of the Statue of Liberty with a few friends
for refusing to leave one night in protest of the United States invasion
of Grenada in 1983, I thought I'd be spending more of these words on feeling

slightly ahead, slightly behind, all the time, in a voice, on tape, on a wall, in a blind
turning at night to keep you awake & followed, you enter the party & are accused
of not being dead, there's no joy in what I like in that mid-life crisis of a rhyme, I can't
prove my father wasn't crazy at the end of his life unknown as an end
if that's what you heard, & assumed I a watchful arriver in the late 90s
had too, was Mel Parnell a good pitcher, you better believe it

look him up & down, shake your head, & walk away, just know where
the trashcan lids are, I never hit anybody for real, though I volunteered
for a punch in the face once, to get some tension out of the way, I try
not to make lists, but Doug knew I was the world's most reluctant
phone caller, California: better than Frank O'Hara, not as good
as Jim Brodey, all the painter bios get slack when the money kicks in
he was just trying to see how many opinions he had, how many onions
a skater might need to melt the underice & maintain the tilted aplomb
of a neurologically fucked up cat, my sixth grade teacher said didn't
your father let himself die, wasn't that a dumb thing for a smart man
to do, but she'd only heard he didn't want to go to the hospital
not that he wanted to die in his bed having said his last words
it will be alright, I know no one believes me in my head when I defend
the way we lived, trust but verify, skunked but very fly, study the avid
picture plane diva smoked out in the mob's balcony, two kids, two cats
two therapists, five part-time jobs, two credit cards, one passport, no
driver's license, two degrees, two umbilical hernia surgeries, one genetic
deficiency, two bank accounts (one joint, one empty)

then Robert Reich tweets that Jeff Bezos' D.C. mansion will have 25
bathrooms & 1,006 light fixtures, then the defining characteristic of Gen
X is wanting everyone to shut the fuck up, damn, I messed up, with all
the numbers, & can another force, I didn't do it, be released, I did it perfectly
into the non-transcript, I did it but incompetently, & be the disembodied
detour we seek to go away, I used to be a stable genius but now I am
getting fucking killed every day, looking at shit from shit's perspective

may not be the way our forceful histories must loom & you miss the little
things recordings say I do, I am sitting in a plum, similar to the one you are
in now, impeach a dirty filthy disgusting word, that anything might be
installed on the instruct I cannot say, I can no longer say where, I cannot
say how long, I no longer remember, I do not know what to make of, I could
hardly have said how, I have only an indistinct notion, nor can I properly
describe, do not know how I got through, and yet whatever idea one has is
always susceptible to doubt's recreation, it's true I painted a Rauschenberg

creep the verb your redux inflames, hiding around perimeters, I mean my
today I got told how oddly, sonic nearness, I'll get paid for a few months next year
Blade Runner now takes place in the present, no, it takes place in absolute time
nowness as projection of a future, we like to bypass relative time in order
to fake the front, the surface, the hard soft face we can't only cover with streams
of sounds affecting shapes that might be words, right about now I should prove
I can betray, fuck, acknowledge, ignore, assault, berate, love, abhor, obey, and die
—please imagine the appearance of a dozen lines in which you can respond
to the merits & absences these choices of descriptor represent, I will go to
therapy tomorrow, couples therapy, become stricken ground, & to the other
therapist to weigh need's possibility the next day: ask me later if these things
happened, I did it, I did the correct version of it the record of its demands

the record's my particular friend, unlike this faceless pressure next door
informing my very brink of a sound by sound shape making life
The New School is competitive with CUNY & Pratt in terms of adjunct
wages for writing teachers, the city surrendered itself to me, I survive
only because I live within this reversal, a baby roachie approaches &
I know it is time to, or begin again, on the outskirts of cents & dollars
the cat's fourth surgery in four years has taken place since I started
& the cave reading beckons, the cave of suicession, Doug's cave, the cave-in
of walk-ins that don't kill yr dreams of post-rent surplus to pop off with
for five unsurveilled seconds, the camera's in your pants & memory's the dealer
we've replaced memory with the future still, having agreed to be seen & scenes

once in a cave I just took a picture of this page which you are not
experiencing as page, page boy, or paige mead, & posted it & a few
pages prior as pictures of poetry in process to prove or maybe just show
I can open the sketch in public but you'll have to break out yr x-ray
magnifying zoom-in super bouncy eyeball to read this horrible hand
writing, moving around a blank-faced drawing I'm betraying as image
to keep free of mess & message, though I'm a photograph of bad at cleaning
a failure at the controlled touch, & a private admirer of the eternally ruined
waves of jaywalking clamor dolled up as squalor, I believe only in the public
budless self-talkers, among all these destructive concessions to respectability

the last dude who hired me could not only not tell me how much the job paid
but wasn't authorized to know, that's life in American education for you
twisted in the taillights to maintain flakefulness, I think I better have one more
& go, go pick up the kids & get them uptown to the cave, to Jimbo's chili, which they
won't eat, and the promise of unrecorded voices spiking the 21st century's script
of a derailed collective nervous system, I hope to make it to 49, to have these pangs
and pangs of pangs adopt a less rote psychological dread zone, I have always
felt some sense of deficit as strength in relation to poetry and living, & looked
for ways to close the gaps in advance of their less sophisticated replacements
hovering externally as forms of blunt knowledge & tethering voices performing
negation as a fantasy of withdrawal from life, we know the surfaces are poisoned
but I believe underground in a yes where these forces of inevitability can be shed

Poem in the Manner of Civilization

If one could call catharsis
an emotional space we wanna
not knock over the work here
I was thinking about plumbing
a facility for deadpanners
to fulfill your thinking in my
mind really summons sitting
on the toilet flattening the
cylinder I missed part of
the intro because I was at the
vending machine which seemed
to have that duck-rabbit
ambiguity I miss tuning
that fungal quality of taking
a shower on psychedelics &
the red carpet anguish of a B
movie star in a not good
outfit as a constant firehose
of labor affects the too-muchness
of the world, the strange way
the deconstruction of fake
memories from historical
truth wonders what level
of awkwardness the story
should maintain, though the
reveal of the arrangement
is very slow, & this feeling
of being a broken mechanism
wants it to make it its own
bumper, more in the logic
of objects, & then I was thanked

for having been the undoing
of a voice on but not activated
the strange way we go together
makes me feel as if I'm supposed
to feel we're barely holding on
to shivness, some weird spiral
which makes sense in terms
of you, making you see fast
if there's really anything more
domestic than a dog painting
& the strange things that makes
people say, & then I reject
access to focus on commentary
feeling less and less the need
to express myself under the
habit of imposing every
sign, in a hotel room, going
to work, always getting ready
to appear, it's funny that I's
partial quality must always
take reaffirmation medicinally
& though there is no general
public I fist bump with this
one old pal because arthritis
which agrees with the last thing
said, seeing bodies too, but
maybe not human bodies
one of my favorite things to
do when I go into a house
is go into the basement, little
clay objects ask what complicates
barring brutalist surgery, an
inner life, these rocks too
can gain infamy, & I really

like the round heads, the
round-headed kids' delib-
erate speaking tempos up
against the local wall
the future citadel will
pull back its floor as the
sun goes zombifying into
the west, under the weight
of evidents, said some surly
notation in a fit of tenor
authenticity is a label, a true
screen comes out of a belief
in the after more than the
next, in translating myself
I become formal with
myself, the resurrection
is about human fulfillment
the material archive of the
spirit, or art, the sentence
is a moral unit, a formalist
fantasy of not having a
body & the desperation
the dude says is in all
certainty, a lot of easygoing
failure the camera has
been released from thought-
making where the stress
goes is mitigation when
desire is fully dictated
by demand perhaps
the refracting thing
could be pushed more
& why don't I question
the age of the piano?

Wobble Factory

broken noseling glides on air, bloken exhaust
giggles orange warbler onto solitary stair
grab a cadillac & toss it on its back
to impeach the solitary sandpiper we must
& do some high rise erasure around
Manhattan disappear the 59th st. bridge
wipe Moses from the map
impeach that shrieking cardinal
conversations with trees plagiarism maps
costume education deficit
reducer daddy-o truncation's
boyfriend behind glass breaking itself
an evolved & informed cynicism sharing
face with digger as they
say of that crazy beat: total redacted
exoneration with flexible figurines & we
can see each other through
our particle shafts, *they* mean
masks, but *we* only communicate
through colonial type, to
bike in this town you must
radically break lazy laws
to survive I almost like
this poem enough to stop
as handwritten
photograph last night I
shared some family trauma (*again*)
only have good days I tell myself
when I see
a cormorant (impeach

the cormorants) new
inverted elevator shaft
for throat all alone
like Starbury sneaks in the sum time, gotta
impeach the glimpse
just on this bench
cause I thought Marina's paintings on
bowery were on 94th
of Sunday drives on weekdays
present frame of line: reactionary
unqualified   and stuff

* * * * *

anticipating a violence that's always coming's
how much recourse it takes to build
this janky non-immersive world
rescuing dino eggs to bring back to 30th
century cultline with virtual hop there's
something oddly devotional about this thinsulate
rear intent disempowering
itself from at least both sides
painting notation into your unfinishable thought
but in the process of creating imbalance
ambiguity & suspicion something
strange happened, I looked
forward to future melancholy
the weed roach pulled the install
together, the other room agreed with
the fake screw, gestation constantly
deferred to the future
the desk an ungiven . . .
so as to maintain remorse, & work
no one's really thinking about, yes,
hi, marina, exploring imaginative possibilities
with the word fake, the pink here
for natural light, the "insight"
reality's a boring & unreliable friend
M says what's a photogram, asking the flesh
the paint directed toward flesh spreading
in shivers, the implicated buddy
improper edges to things fly up, and out, rather ripped
I'm in the exhaust, scathering wheres gattered
I will make this about me to enable me

to help you: a pedagogy
colonic perforation from over there opening
a crass display of medium-well ephemerality wiring
receives orange unavailability, as light
broken foot, no money, can't work, soon dye
the neutrality unquote of flowers, complicated
to bounce off, Alex thinking about signifiers of courtship
sweet & tender access, when I was here alone I had
a very different experience the projection
sucks off seduction, today the day of the causal plunge
this little guy is called comfort hole
the two-sided plungers become lollipops
back to huddle presence, maps of presence
full compartmental spree café
under an obtuse if polite barricade

* * * * *

applause performed only in fist bumps
why does your desire for language always
manifest conservatively in private
o hustler of accessibility
a little gold-painted stapler
to staple pages for bugs together forever
the cups *should* be a photograph
the studio goes outside for a stroll
but there is no sidewalk, no path
no concession to the plight of the pedestrian
& yet one goes on looking for signs
of life on foot in Cookeville eating rows
of crumpled napkins, an honest emission
trapping thinking & tricking it into
the feeling of release, in public in pocket
I do know you're ready to think for me
they do well with friends, the thoughts
others want you to have, a little to the side
of art historical expectation
is this inviting illegibility so threatening
from across the room Anselm Berrigan
did Petsfit Dogs Carrier Backpack for
Cat/Dog/Guinea Pig/Bunny Durable
& Comfortable Pet Bag meet
your expectations better & cheaper than
humane complicity a brand's tactic to live
in montage time during real time to
create the overlay of commonality

to mudwrestle or soilwrestle with
the assumption of commonality
the necessary calcification of the greater good
oh Kevin!
a painted bottle of leaves
floats out into the center room
ruined into possibility
by words
I have to love how many tones
you let make use of you
in order to move at all

* * * * *

dodo money powder
cat horsie flies
mice flowers rose, t
ree hair rock nose
dirty eyes
pretty teeth powder, wind nap uck
toes, ick feet doodoo hands fuck ear, meat baby food
bear candy bear dope sparrows
solitary band name got no when to when with
crime is the feather in which we urne
we actually had a deal & then they broke it OK
used to it, done it many times meself
either shit's special everywhere
or we stop making reservations in imaginary places
I don't have any seeds for you sparrow
I don't know what to tell you midway
through dubious incredulity ting that far
an enormous truck suddenly hurled
a good professional ing imagined ining formed
into horrors, the transcript
is now live, it contains but can't stop
our second indifference, our recorded indiffigbars
trend to turn whitewashed flock affairs
in scrollight deposition, laying head in lap mode
of grass & the deep give off grass dreams about
the ways sacks dream of sackable partners
bean to fleck, in rotographic memory of
reelings, hey
dopey, hand me that hand

* * * * *

history by implication nuzzles in fragments
as an anti-resonance machine
a problem in recording
a hidden record of soil bummer
if dreams are just personal fantasy spaces
tamed by interpretation I can't just rip up
the cardboard box and put it behind glass
I have to describe that getting done so I cut out
x-men: dark phoenix works
Alex says
it deals   with trauma & pedagogy   speaking of
one sentence film reviews language contains an infinite
array of bullshit as source / who bleeds poetry
the foundation for
most dreams an instability
specific to experience, no shit
proximity on the wing hijacks
the performance poor plicit
always serving the pre-fix they liked
we better they liked me better when I was
the shyest shade of alive
in that dream she slipped under
the wheel don't want to serve sense
the difference
between accident & intention the greater the bleed
bloat to ritual the story
disarmed by light to require
aid in making decisions
butt tree capillary séance
a recording of a potato chip

a slow decay of appreciation for infinity
something technology can actually *do*
I was thinking a lot about the
certainty *the* implies with
precarity in attempt
at the non-sexist
surreal the ghost of
commendation hiding
inside a protest's memorial
I heard some human activity & had
to bend down low
to the ground's shadow
itself a feint at figure's grief
& all that affluent flatness
to follow

* * * * *

live in the agency of self-deprecation, just to mean
differently, one another after the other, I wish I could
have gotten what it was not to know what was ongoing
to ongone the scroll refuses, as form, encapsulation, sinister
splayful & gruff, devious echo-ed & fluff, really small
comment, you didn't put out a floor for us, the way
surveillance enhances our experience of loneliness, or
that I am uninterested in being further smothered by
a certain spurious sensitivity, & who is the projection
of if not the self in multiples, what if, death aside, we're
not doomed, or, ungone, is doom underrated overrated
or properly rated, bent pipe sticking out of calm lake
water is so loaded, can't say I make work for the survivalist
community, I can't remember if preemptive self-criticism
is more of a pre or post 9/11 phenomenon, what with
all the conversation we no longer get to have, & now
disjunctivised, sitting's too hard, even when pushed down
into the future manifesting as carcass, is it or them
manifesting or masquerading, is the masquerade art, is
is what is means, goddamnit mr. 90s, growth is terrific
unless you can't get rid of it, though alienation may be
a new form of relic I do believe in Reverdy's yes, even
if the last year in particular, blubber's dripping on the
bystand, been pretty rough, a buzzer sound furevah
doesn't have to be bamboo, a bunch of things inside
a tube, to get beyond sets of choices as a proportion
of surface batting around this identity construct, an

inversive threat, a target as a late mask, an early task
of tearing into finishing, I wish upon you what I wish
upon nobody, a scale that is out of your control, &
that truckload of paraphernalia that would burden you
to be overly conscious of, don't you think two minutes
on the enigma/fantasy scale, is a little short for a tribute?

* * * * *

I wanna hear more about how you feel
about space: well, prose governs the forms
of compliance, swishes, slys & sdreams, sub-themed
woofer sneaking up from behind, what's real:
the instable fundament
at the disappearing root of nothingness:
slather, slosh, uncross your unlegs, unbegs, his or his bags
& having a conversation with the spaces between
passing bodies, we are unlikenesses
unpoised to strike out in or on
the current version of unpremises upon
which half-shaved dogs pant along imitating
gaily breezing as the phones walk their humans
we love not reading the mail we live
to doofus mainlines stepped away from
her office at home they feels like a seminal
tourist in pocket of da bus only zoneliness
So I Duck ruffled and wrapped
in draperies dreaming in front of
a geometric portal between self-deprecating
family portrait with tipsy special guests
& funerary bearafters, bear bare rafters
a harried minded pink flared boar, it's
the out of fashion notebook poem coming to
bite yr ass from multiples temporal
locations on bear's head at twice
& thrice you gnarly potluck

you vicious grimace in the quay
you constant embowled neglector
of oversight and overstock & squeaky
singing twins in the fields of nihilism
you're about as ironic as the real in real
dick, you're contemned to be a serious
afterlife, you're a principled casual touch

*****

kind on that note
the permission transaction
you better beeeeee there
the stand in projects the certainty of
the passion of
the replacement
the propping of the scenic
the authoritarian consolation of symmetry
I don't have any details about it
I'm very quoty this year
I think about dying every day
attempting to touch history with a tuning spork
one bye one bye one bye one bye one buy one tone get free for
three, moves thoroughly through disidentification, I'm
the courtroom doll demanding fealty
to induced abjection
courtesy of maleficient prelease of live male experience
explerience of the angry male gesture
to derange your memory
to tame back into the realism I project, the iris is a muscle
I just heard, on a high alert
unfortunately I'm actually aging into your projection
of a comprehensive detachment
it ain't true, but you know
the only bandwidth that matters
decides otherwise, compliance
is no outward necessity in this assemblage
we call country, there shall be no Anselm in the future
used to be clarity but now am certainty
used to be alone with the work, so now, trashed chemistry

crowded pocket life, look, if you can't give encouragement
to a poet, are you really there
yield, debris, target, iris, ache, moan, stammer, fervor
attract, hang, chuckle, hole, some say performing the inter-
view creates a counterabyss, one which must be trained
to love, some say that highly trained squads of lovemakers
may leap from the hoax & fulfill their destinies
to use doubt against immobility
the contours of the abyss may be a friend
though it's dangerous to reduce friend to portal
you're lying it's true, & the baby clowns see you
but, you know, fuck all those broadcasters
looking like fake people

* * * * *

just the layeredness of that
I can't tell support
about your desire to be right
like tracked sound   do you make the things
I want to keep, I'm a ghost
in your imagination, haunting streets
you cannot believe real, yet there is no
permeability here, & I
remain a very real site of pre-sent
character, holding up a wall
in the room of integrated arts, feets
sore brain hardly working
ready to convert notation
into need, to fight back your practical
onslaughts of vocabulary
competing realisms come down on being
stuck here, with me, right, Miko?
the tension is drips
dripping drippingly, the reader wants
a hug
& what will define for me an idyll
beyond looking it up, usually think of reptiles
or maybe spiders
the good news is a large shipment of bamboo has
arrived, our surfaces objects our objects surfaces
lying to perimeters, lying to unreliability
lying to the reference dying to be an influence
lying to the studio & the creepy old mask guys

        & the frozen mice in waiting   & then we desire
      implication as a manner of speaking, now I
 can finally own something unreal
  a floor's distortion of a ribcage, through
       which the brackish grawk premonition I once was
   once myself   & then came to driving backwards
through a tunnel

 if only standardized means of   submission weren't
     delicately pervasive octopi   bobbing in cryptivity

* * * * *

narrow bridge with fraught fundamentals caught
between the pre-disparaged & the post-effusive
the heron & the bishop on rented bloom
bored with participation
a project without production
or process or abscess or incest
with a skirmish at the oasis
there were elements of deadly
dull historical importance
have a nice visibility
have a fabulous mobilization
storm your own private winter palace
in public factory sinews a flag's futility
a lust for the hostile audience
an artificial place in hell takes itself to the theatre
did Kaprow ever eat that hershey bar
was Cage ever untied from the bed
were the highly trained squads of lovemakers
ever highly trained
& sent out
to make love
to the police
got the money
but not the benefits
the grooved approximation
of being there
will replace your objects
eventually, the populist wing
of a cultural arm
if you're going

to be a nominalist
be an awesome nominalist
scratch the little pixel
& make it come up
you're a genius shower
of slides to boot, please don't
come here, please don't
please don't be here
please self-selectively disappear
please give in
please recede, or initiate
a process of receding
please let the wolf feed on you
before we re-remove
the wolf from view

* * * * *

razor days await
the equivalent
of not leaving
tenderness vendettas
training face
entraining
faces north
don't reveal sources
the earth already
overrun by citation
revision equals dread
I hate notifications
response is one of many
divisions of representation
alls turning out
to be looked at
inconsequentially
constantly, blurry angels
on M's back, silent for now
if you don't hear me sorry
I'm not good at projecting
pre-durational awkward
shot length, grotesque fire
do you enjoy the stuck
feeling of watching things
burn or work, Jesus let
the rope go and his figure
remained suspended

in the foreground
in the movie theater
not in the film
in progress
the unbelievable real: deer
ticks in renderable paradise
hints of amorphous whiteness
occur to the speaker
in next to nature, fantasy
seems to replace anxiety
yet one is a form of the other
at any point, a minor deviation
who needs poetry
it's a total misreading
of that shot, oil, canvas, string, acrylic

a wet thread playing
at transnational object

we cannot conform to
the spatial logics
we know well
the mood data we project
as personal splice factory

express, express, express . . .

*****

sounds moving shape shapes the unforgiven
devil chapbook
dj ashtrae living in
his sister's bathroom, I really need
I really need, a pair
of two-tone jeans
for question cleaving
(brandish internalized scythe!)
made a purple
speech & its speech
balloon cried
farting at the reading brother mask
makes the slip
to give itself
Fernando vs Rags
no charts no
tests, no punctual
punitive identifications, no
sour features, olives
are so good J only has to say
& there's the poem
but which in fact *only*
degenerates can make homages
truly, the seamstress
seems to want to reinvent flying
while she futzes with the electronics don't let the sun
deceive you
amused on extinctions latest verge
a uniformal verge drenched in ichor, a blank
tap to play we must barricade the literal

with Bernhard's sports car
bopped S with my
pen on her forehead touched
the bottom of the chill pill
each thing said
only happening to someone else, each thing
said a moon in a trunk
mishandled across the way
each thing said's got
its own abandonment
principle trained holding
up your trousers
with extension cords

* * * * *

humans are much more interesting when they're open about
what they don't know, or at least *my* I thinks that's the case
working centimeter by centimeter, expression admitted
but cordoned off, recognized & defanged, breaking
against the dismantling of real strangeness, idiosyncrasy
& unpredictable defiance, this profound solemn occasion
is also incredibly boring
the gravity, the conscience, the unwavering
attention to that which is severe
& poorly rendered in the names, change sub-theories
fall out of local vat, hang two bobbing
don't do that actually, don't
actually, don't, peace sign flashed
across way to lantent
bening (latent benign) enemy
how go public with the after
all of existence, the planet isn't dying it's
getting rid of us
I put the rubber dragon
the green yellow white superball
of river lines, the soapstone zebra
the amethyst regular
rock, the sharp fossil eddy
& the poem in tied up book
on the purple
Poetry Criticism volume
for all the fellows
in the fellowship to write out of &
semi-freely ignore, dead link publishing

& if you're so smart how come
sophisticated & trained
you're not poor
your scales
not nearly as intrusive
as your feathers
let us disembark from
the parenthetical
the monetization
of our righteous unknowables
needs blown into the suture
of the human goldfish action, I
imagine a motto of moratoriums

lunch or suicide: a review question, a violet fall off
a non-horse, why know more than what is said
about what was said the world of real estate pleads
for more real amidst the granulation's deregulation
you want to wait on spicy off bears arse, the whole
fragile structure wobbles into picture planes, our
platformed degradations when all that is is another
malleable concept, another front for giving in, don't
you need to be prepared in the conversation you're
uncomfortably having with the wind
which wishes to be named, when my brother
punches you, with a fist full of roaches, I wonder
if the correct response will resonate eternally
before selection is forced upon me, I wonder if
I talk about myself secretly and now must o
weep if not parenthetically then between the streets
Keats was a traumatized ocelot who predicted tv why
is my little man shaking I should glow better

*****

uh-oh all of too many wounds lights pointing down
replace pleasing with truncated replace challenging
with god gave you a clue, replace future get out
some withs say, when probability shall be no more
deep adaptation, the favor of ruining
American poetry face to faith & limb
say you hope this musical
performance of dominature hurts
speaking to the obliged, with medicinal care
in search of a non-corrosive precarity
expecting me to talk, how many well to do
oinks will do, Jesus is paying me
to produce opinions, I love little
pages in the dark, empty downtowns
in big cities stripped of civic possibility
I love perforations in edibility
pink light scoring background shadows
into fonts of debt-ridden documentation
but don't get all archivey on me my tender
anchovy of blood glove for free
now we can only write when being paid to do other things
let it look like notation: a performance of
attention & bitchin' thought-extension no one says
bitchin' in poems no more
I'm overqualified for
the New York School, total use of you
inner tube frames mirror, little guy junior
in drawn baggy lines, pachyderm on napkin
pinned to wall, between table & leg of

model travels out & up, adding to itself
with raindrops & spit, chipmunks
protest grandeur, I can't keep tracks, I submit
dumbly to each given experience
in order to estrange myself into engagement
I have to type this up before nature steals
my inexplicably said yes, and again
dog dog dog, why why why
the will's scores of shalls walks
into the local frame shop
giving off that just fucked look

* * * * *

the figure in my dream collapse was like what
about a kazoo, we don't wanna thank anyone
we've outsourced gratitude, or maybe we've
insourced it to ourselves, to our deliberately
inauthentic politics which we mainly project
onto coexistence but so it's avant-garde because
it has definition, it being a complex of orificially
genuine feints at trashy sensuality aghly we bought
you here to participate in the not knowing what
we're talking about, it's a complicated issue which
I'll tell you about later, after the lasers, beekeepers
& torchbearing children have finished flipping
process into procession, it's unclear as of yet
whether, when at a q & a, it's the q or the a
that sees you, in the audience, picking your nose
precisely at the moment when you reach your brain
& begin to rearrange, though we really need to
consider the performance of the bedbugs, removed
from the bed, confined to the artist's bedless studio
the foil set against, before discovery, before extermination
before the evaporation of the spectator, before projects
for projects' sakejects in the sunject, the fluidity of
remarks as the basis for ending critique, as we know
Adornal Urino, one adores total angsters, from a
necessary sub-middle distance, is there an elephant
in *any* room, I can hear a crow outside, above, it
persists, the problem with the block is its insistent
circulation, its gravity, its context retains shape as its

surface goes blank, rambling productive crow
why'd that dude in the corner act like a dick, common
metaphor alert, thought without record, the fugue in
the dream-exploited reentry above is the mouth for
a wicked organ, the overwrought incursions of personal
history, lying behind the curtain of words, a boppity
strain, I've no longer met a truly, wings cling, clear frame

*****

the smart friend explains that we never really touch
when we touch, nice knot knowing the extremes
of uncertainty's extremity, pick of friction spread
out in front of a trembling body cut into music
the off be in charge, what you do with hyperventilation
for beginners, grace to beat bronze
out of brazen whispers
the strict devil's advocate feels up more
constraint than the casual devil's
advocate, whose interests
are more internal, this phantom limb thing
brought up in the room as form of investment
the um is tradition, not the phantom trad-magic
I wish the shrouded by baby blue comforter
figure had no front, elegant & revferential
choosing materials post-destined to fail prophecy
I type as the cats in unison
vomit at home
something somehow separation earth
is also a terrarium I am curiously
alienated from the slick hapticness
of your camera insulation, insulation
foam, drywall, two bye fours, jumping off
on that theatrically D's thinking a lot lately
about who gets to do what
it being itself, takes a fragile feel
for dislocation to render captivity
L's excited by things rotting
from the inside out, I guess I will be too
R senses a mediumness, going with

the giant diamond
having pierced the desk, & I
I give in to letters w/ a craven overtness
that's what I/we figure, E has
met the orb people
who believe in orbs, & that
Samuel, is what we do when we
letterize names

for Samuel Breslin

* * * * *

when we met we talked about what it is to observe
& over here we encourage you to breathe
to not be that chased rabbit
running around the perimeter
of your studio, I don't like
long atmospheric slides
into a level horizon either
the cost of eggs on her mind
up and staves, bones olives masonry
insight fret all level rotation
introversion is the only pure
form of self-destruction left, to keep away
from this addiction to hooks, disturbing twist
is a title you should obviously use, arch logistics
if any such they had
watching Dora pop back into animated head
in an unburning Amazon
windshield: every (there is no) windshield is
its own point of view
canvas model perspective nonstop, I close my eyes
hey little numbers floating away
I see a red flickering at the center of
an orange & yellow I put there
to take to target & buy & drop
& buy & drop, out of a Vivian Springford painting, & cue
you up to polite voices, the flickering is a portal
to prove memory's not my complete enemy, what's up
with that summer humumus, which I am allowed to witness
but not enter, did you know we're everybody's enemy, & memory
I walk the wealthy streets that were broken streets, canvas is bricks

you're never ok with the snapshot, with the, with all the little thes
leading into listening, lending listening to a who gets to let
themselves talk to you, hey cutoff, hey hydrant, hey fin blowing
up to our feet, hey Dolphy, hey Molly Adams talking to me
like neighbors talk when being close is private sounds
through the walls we pay something to share
we're talented at leaving little lists along the way
if I can't do evil you can't do funky I had to say to J
talking about types of sorbet

* * * * *

the best dork defender, an atomic bomb aesthetic
the feedback of our bodies, the nesting of cubes
are you in an open relationship with yourself
she's reading from the audience chair position
I think I need to make this higher
S gets the honorary most improved award
which uh, that one, the improvably most
honorary award award, I need to dye one eyelash
purple, the tug of responsibility, I don't, I don't
know what I'm doing, *you* may have known
this for a long period of time, but *I* only
just found out, & it'd be pretty liberating if
I weren't so "tired," even if I'm just
imitating people who are *really* tired
I mean, deadpan neutrality works
in the crypt, and I'm actually rather optimystic
when not oppohectic, but I consider
optomysticism & melancholy to be
symbiotic, in the field, where I am making
these recordings, between plateaus
and scrubs, Sylvie said she didn't really think
TLC's No Scrubs was about not wanting
to take a bath, but she said that, & left me
being looked at, which is something
to imitate, like I was the customer copy, & not
the merchant copy, & then to walk around
town with the words "amount deposited"
just below where you put the coins in me

before making a selection was almost
too much, and in the evaluation process
I was inferred I mean I was the model
looking out at the painter, & not
that narcissist the viewer, photo for wing win
going to be later for dinner
because I'm completely filling this page
which I promise not to change, with writing

JOHN COLETTI
IMITATION RACKET

Find My

back by the bridge
facing Brooklyn above
my oversized page   sipping
the dour-handed juice with
a cormorant's turquoise eye
& a stranger's grizzly smile
I wonder who the fuck am I
to be here now alongside
traffic & current & disease
& I know exactly what I am
barelife undrawn
mask down & mask on
Justice's floaties & probes lingering
in the mental byways
I cut with sky—can I write
like Coletti monster once
for future times' shake ?
béisbol, grant me the
anonymity the marbled warbler
cosplays, no one gets
to get decisions made
no one's decisions
no

please keep it concise

as when process
releases intuition

from assignation

what you need

to not know

in order to begin

with everything

happening to you

(one or two minutes
unintelligible)

Are you scared of corners ?

Sleep paralysis
for studential
consumpt

masked song

pre-face
dancer

the commission
on murder
& equity

would like
to like
a word

John Coletti Zoom Meeting

End of book

Thanks human

Hop ho hop

Theraflu's caribou

Meeting adorations

Masked on the inside

why, arrow?

redtailed baby

hawk practicing

hunting pigeons

to the bleat

The Maintains

of alrightness

the Montaignes

of alightness

the refrains

of smiteness

the muse & drudge

outskirts us

j.c. imitation #2

rice is rice for the most part

rice is like universal

there are things comedians say

do they know the fire's perimeter

like we do not do

sinkhole that applears

apple ears

slinkhole in arrears

nominally

(tentative all-defense)

"I've never felt older

than anyone

I've outlived"

(said with Joseph Carey, 6/25/20)

*****

A: "Will you be voting in the election on Tuesday?"

B: "No, I'm an anarchist"

A: "Then this conversation isn't going to go well"

B: "if I did vote it'd be like
in Chicago: early & often"

A: backing away, smiling . . . . .

smooth sleuth meets the slooth smeuth

sparrow
high pipe feral bites I chihuahua
low wheels spicy betray nose
cheeto & all fuzz
flies who pink
no longer off in compliment
than no a panic me

Pet shop eyes the growlers
the copters compass the
marchers the gallup polls
the Christians swallow flies
In Circles—dogs in band—
anas—dashes in flitter
masks—grease applies
numerously—all our prior
eras finally redesigned!

(that the best you can do?)

directions (content) & shudders
scrolling scrolls back
NYPD SUCK MY DICK
shouted the various teen anti-
traffic marchers—you might
see every murder ever
every murder by cops
of Black people ever in
that video of George Floyd
being murdered by cops
Now what's your definition
of a cop, in American?

*****

ear pause
playing sex
on a french fry
bonapartes gull
resists puppetry
thundercat on audio
the gull backbumps
the air above
air it's already in
bird physics
humble me into
pangs of lust
for strangers
the angle of welcome
tilts away toward
some future promise
of further distance
seagull legs little
little contrast twigs
joggers jog by
& suggest lines
pigeons practicing swallow
routes they can't they
cut hard through
the eulogy brief
competition notices only
its own miscirculation
in this fake summer's
preterformance
this shit better
sound good when
I say it out loud
it better change

take off those
wholly whistling
underpants &
air ravaged tie
sometimes I think
(but not really)
the bathroom sink
clogs itself just
to get me too
stick my fingers
down into it
bobbobbobbobbob
(spackled pigeon
walking by)
well that's actually
a spontaneous
invention of
future animation
honkers glide by
w/ too good posture
fuck it all up
& crack U ok?
Might as well
eat a free chip

You don't say

I have been told
and want to say
all the things I
normally don't say
in that I have to
circumventilate my
ability to articulate
the range of what
could be said &
thereby thought about
(in that I often thing
I only think by talking)
in order to just say
some immediate shit.
& I like not sticking to.
a project or at the vary
least lying my way through
a project's rendition , so as
to at least get put in
position to rhyme rendition
with position before
anything else gets too
alarmed to be sayable

You don't sayeth

That I mean this dude
over here bench right
maskless apologized for
possibly reading aloud
& bothering me the slimy
poet set amidst small
dog yaps at the green
space recently rerevealed
by pandemic flight to
be full of bent homey
locals like it always had
to has been being but
now they're easier to spot
again what's happening
igloo shouldn't your dog
have a mash on too I
would seem to be
practicing faux-response
ability again—I always
do by wirting—& love
likes to tell me so—
you wuz supposed to
be knowing what time
it may be, privacy :
all your personnel
numbers in one
place poetry's terr-
ific all around
game makes look
a little pudgy

You can't soppethy
But I tend to think
of feelings as overlapping
waves in barely
trackable succession
you know, some times
I got to talk to
& the lit sneaks go by
with elevated ice cream
purple lights in circles
down low and the id
already devoured above
"I bought him for
like nine cents" let's
not figure this over
herd out together
cycling through Western
fire's smoke to Brooklyn
that tail's got no
squirrel, Ms. Hawk

You donut slay
This & they pass
with care. If you
want to be exactly
what they pay for
Diplomacy's for
suckers. Disease
Control's for suckers
Sweep that fucking
forest floor. Whose
gonna clean the dirt
that never got on off
my ass? I glove
thee more than Jesus
too , captain. Five
Lights. Bathrooms
everywhere, are
you knocking
over clouds
again ?

I understand & wish to proceed

but am I expected

to perceive everything

as soon as it *happens* ?

“in the early naughts”

Big Sketchbook
Semi-Survival Poems

Like Real People I lent normal
screens of hyper-revenge to
pass through pandemic's end
of the night private zoom party
leaving by copter after the wood's chopped
by a true twisted fact-simile—maybe
its starlessly thyme to give King Crimson
a listen, you were the planet eaters
inn yourn dreamn

Mandy

static (blue)

death understood only

as death's photograph

ha ho he

there is algorhythms

+ subduxction for

them

numerouses

reading aloud

on the inside

that truant

performance

so says E:

lemme
give
you
a
gift
rapt
peanut
Children
of the
New Drawn
(who didn't do
something
screen time wrong)
keeps touching
its face

why wouldn't I
silverlight
stay
cults in full-screen
never quite mode? loose
need words

the budgets
they're need that
prescribed blue shadow
coming down
my nose
(don't touch)

he's got Joe Biden eyes

connection lost

*****

Post-cormorant bar:

do *you* have a rotatable

(primal engagement)

live eye

that can see
360°

(forever unplanned)

in any direction?

(purple bike pedals)

"white space
propaganda
for the poem
itself"

(it's awesome to
watch kids run)

—the poem
in progress

It was fucked
up when naked
St. John the Baptist
all smiley and ambitious
turned into David
holding up Goliath's
severed! head in a Caravaggio
self-portrait

(but I don't care)

or all/none
    of the abyss?

query: should visual
emphasis be added as:
(but *I* don't care)
(but I don't *care*)
(but I *don't* care)
(*but I don't care*)

*****

There's so little to
(spicy honey)
have to do
(thirty minutes)
on weekends
(of Die Hard)
other than dying
(need to watch)

escalators
freeze

I will
if
I can
lift
my hands

(mess
with
me)

unlikability

resides
specifically
here

I always get fluid

write when
I gotta
leaves

In search of . . . .

~~the~~ optimal
balance of detachment
within absolute ordinary
freak out mode
as ongoing barrier
to desired state
of non-productivity

YOU GO GIRL

in big white letters

on the East River's

collection of bullshit

structures

Planet Terror

quarantine splatter

the mirro(u)r inroad to dreams

unfortunately I wrote that

go - go crying

in heavy imitation mode
(always . . .)

deceptive floaters

pickled balls
(scattered)

I'm just cherry
(never -actually-
said that)

what's problematic

we eat brains
but we don't gain

is total global

yr knowledge

pandemic
(not what
you want)

when my mouth
detaches from
brain , delays
ensue & enervate

someone else
is here

choking on the
premise
of future
food

you ever become
that fancy
goal doctor?

I think you're funny

a missing leg
that's now
missing

Last Thrift

The feeling inside
Inside my apartment
Seems to require
Cat hair everywhere
And joyful anxious sick people
Ack! Am I
Careening?
Pandemically & pregrettably yours, yes, pickled
We plotz, blips to loop
An empanada from
The throngified bikeways
Thwacked with zombified droplays.
I did glove that empanada
In a hospicity, cuz
My borrowed blue bandana's a portal to zebraic
Tenderness.
So I flame on.
And splay hlome.
And bug out discretely
Bumming antennae from broken bodies.
Sometimes the roachies in the wall
Mutter in disbelief at the
Notion Purple Rain was Prince's
Idea of a Bob Seger imitation
And pour from invisible cracks
To form a giant crystal question mark
That refuses to writhe or scurry
With a shadow broken into a grin
From which some golden egg
Tempera paint is flowing, bypassing

Daemons to form a ladder made of bluebells
And the tigers are recovering, and the girls
Are inspecting the pink fire escape for slants of light
And inside the hairy Siberians, Nesh & Frankie
Embody a nodding question, furry spoon by furry spoon

for Ron Padgett

Times are dangerous !

you might wake up

into on going danger!

& be surrounded by people

who've been going through danger

longer than you've had a thought

hey, myself

may your imitations

never recede

as you keep trying

to make yourself

possible

4/15/20

*****

moon lunar hallucinations
shouldn't always

cray ven

have to come
with accidents

wake up blowdy

hounded by smiley can openers

even cleaned the sump pump

with micro meteorites

stilgargettting an F3 error

just to cheek
& jettison
the exterior
shell (& replace w/ 5 more! !!)

saran rover wraps
in quarter tones
(Wasn't Me / was my clone)

when you save yourself
standing buy
however (wrong eighthith word)
inadvertently

we could
run
some tests
(for to make obscene hello)

the clone

wouldn't take (not without prior
suggestion)
care of the plants

when we spleak
to each (no connection
(currently)
other)

*****

forgive the
exceptionalism
but it's hard
to believe
we ain't got
all the stupid
here in the

post attendee in zoomster manner

which
whoa
I meant whoa
But it got changed to which

STATES

Delivered

de-livered

Man-thing

thoughts

"hi-ate-us"

I despise myself
for developing

a relationship with

saying

"bandwidth"

It's just been a few
times. A mild pandemic
effect is loss of vocab.

How's things?

That sometimes
was the past three
minutes

Sometimes I wonder
about urgency & where
that overlaps with
constipation

*****

brought to bears

(line produced by pandemic default mode: I
always end up playing around with bears)

this constant resurrection is so alienating

(line produced by pandemic default mode:
built around resurrection & colloquial's *so*)

forgive me default exceptionalism:

(line produced by deadpan pandemic default
mode, which I will (unintelligible: bisect?) in a minute; also
built off another tweet—in fact it was part
of a tweet response: "Ack, forgive my deadpan . . .")

today I stand six ft apart from myself

(popular!)

(full drawn line across page goeth here)

this is—this
~~hab~~ has been a
pain in the ass
to write. It will

not work typed up.
It will have bogus
affect as photograph.

May 27
2020

*****

"junky kitty wants
that fancy feast"

(4 K on her birthday)

this performance it lives on

of anxiety as a shock to

we rough the system even though

here abjure ye sound
(not <u>ye</u>, but YE)

like ye

under
water

can
I
make
you
a :J
throne
for
me?

swim
stamina
yellow
buoy(s) turtle head
pokes up

I

hops in

the heart

shower (subway)

with

thee

denim petroleum pillows!

"NO."

*****

the singer sings
like a man
with long experience
making babies cry

2A "personality crisis"
entirely handwritten

2020
reintroduces
bystanders to gutters

there's no point in tasking
you'll get snow's reply

life on the street
feels more accurate
when we wear
our masks

I realize this "means"
I have "problems"
& need "help"

the guitar sounds great
until the singer starts in
"Yr Daddy works / in porno . . ."

but do you know
anyone inside
yrself who doesn't?

this is a sealed
off statement

gross malpractice

charity

articulate swipe

platform amalgam

what cannot quite

be found

is what we say

we promise

*****

I've done my all
I've done all my wall

stuff   scoff   slought
free retribution

from from's from
the anti-preposition
meets & deletes
(slelf's) elf shelf

the mural is capital letters on re-paved
ave gravel
"meh-rage"

I think I'll be a little late

forever   chemo-sabe

a terrible singing voice
goes by

as anti-menace

flock or fluck
for t-shirt rhythm

you are concerned
with white fragility

but what should

parent(hetical) rump

really scare

curves

yr lack of sleep

is white urgency

impeach the

cormorants

*****

(get your ass
to mars)

don't worry
it's self-guiding

(the Martians
love Kuato)

& since the air
volume is limited

the head removed
predicts

("I don't give you
enough
information
to think")

its own
explosion

only the asides
control the logic machine

(cause otherwise
I'll erase
your
ass)

in that dream hand
sanitizer
became
ejaculate

(you are hereby
asked
to ask
a question)

up your recall

murk plonk foos in toah ree

& rant (sadmin)

unbegrudges granules
stitchedly on vegetative
states panting sleeve

& El Duque was buying jeans with Andrei
& Allen & Peter were back talking
about God a lot

& Breathlahem was
almost distracting from
every cuddly insect in
the world showing up
on this or that leg

what's with all the teen hawks
about you gotta be ready
for something dead falling
out of the local elms

Breathlahem, I rip thee off
Breathlaheh, thy radiant coocloon
cooclone
coclone
cooloony
cicadia
disemergence

& someone emails
to set up a zoom
about another bard
problem

these flies are way
too attracted
to me

through
choked (or cloaked)

shagnificence

*****

got (have)

gut have tooth?

(hare)

crawled on yesterday (it)

crowded under yesterdaze

can't

unmute

won't

? you reallly think

you're gonna pack

for the underground ?

micro - calcifi

- cations feint

working cations

a reflection

back

blow on

yr pinched

nerve

flaketime

(out of)

fuck the probable

or be fucked

probably

fooooooooont

when you love me (our rent is rent-free)

*****

They all sound g
r
i
They all sang everything (n)
Up to now's through d

As I not as at alls
Cook tear
of a some that

shit's not

a curse

or
shit's not
a cursor

either

don't mean
lasing that what const-
ellation—spilling cloven
a thing I won't lose it—
Me & the devil greens
Interventions beg
Years for intro-
Conduction! As
Much Lateness
As youair im-
Pagination can hold
Your yourrair

Horse corset lords people
Lending to bash odd their
Descree musty devil have
Now we have to de- uses
Scribe a nlice gluy
You seet it comet to
Theet & MyExplosiveHeert
& then & then & then (re - served)

*****

poetry —— " creates a grammar
that doesn't exist
to address things
that haven't been
contains addressed " — Hoa
multiple
unresolvable
questions

A T

T H E

SLA ME

TLI ME

*****

The bird watchers tap their lenses
& canes. Junkie or blood donor I
say they thing they say to not me.
Everythink's brilliant. when everyone's
an idiot, language says, for itself
a unified idiocy with toes & guns
& no auntie-freedome masksss. Masks
& yoga pants. Skasers II: a proplosal.
A proplosive to insplosive cross-country
e-pithany for the abject glimpse that
powders love with scurrilous realist
anxiety. Mo fo mo. Do hawks really
cry this much when the food's always
out of range in performance? Still
the worldlings demand schedules to
pretique. Prettique daemonly!!
Begged by text to digitally draw.
Of course I put pigeons in here I
write outside they're anywhere's
punctuation here with twists of
oil puddles wrack & bob. They
fuck in front of me whenever
I'm writing poetry in the park.

*****

your
spayment
sposted

so humid I hat
I had to wipe
my face
with a paper bag

there are
no accidents
in poetry
either
you tell
told
that
fatherfucker

(for Jack Whitten)

we drip
r(e)efer drip
to dripping
the on
out my
of blue
hand mask

It is burst.

(for Johannes)

air calligraphy
(by Hoa)

the buildings around
this expensive grass
I am refusing
to sit on
are far
too tall

see, what you
don't know & I
don't know is
how untrustworthy
I am to the
local architecture

that dog's ears combined . . .
bigger than its head

gotta get better
at them parenthellipses

not down
with
the running air bag

what the fuck
is going on
in Portland?

our shite's exposed
have to handle it
have to unhandle it
at the same time

baby, don't
inherit
your daddy's
current expression

(addressed
to baby
in stroller
just pushed by. Dour daddy
looking sturdily ruined)

cloudy publicity agent

t-shirt clairvoyance

my name is Geraldine

Geraldine Ferraro

I know why my hands are shaking

" an abstraction of dissent

needs to be named

& practiced

as a contribution

to the traditions

of Black radical imagination ”

—Torkwase Dyson

Evelyn bikes by
sees me without
my (blue) mask on

rain in the notebook
brakes the humdittidy

all that booty

the looooooong shoot
w/ latinate
explanation

beyond your capacity
to trust

nope nope nope nope nope nap nap nope nope nope nope nope nope nope nap nope nope nope nope nope n

*****

works to the left
deftly suck—cold
jam session on the   I too am wondering
pink, with the downy
attributes I suffer   which planes
to like, life in the
open office of covid   to stash
detention—but we
growl outside chucking   in the desert   in the dessert
apple bits in the
easterly river afore   in the mouth
affordable kick out   to sneeze within
damn, that building   a disturbance
went from brick brown
to angelic orange by   " confused agency "
the light invested in   speaking of feats
cyclical stomp aplomb
wonks bereft of aarp-
lication supplicate   " a dream " says Cedar
casually in the rivets
you've got the count   in a poem
me ins irregardlesslyness
& he gave away the   " is not necessarily
secrets to his past
& said I've lost control   assigned one body"
(again) rise rise rise
Done by the forces . . .
There's gotta be a
Non - handwritten way
Out of work tomorrow

Marcella D. reading—8/16/20—K/S backyard—Hastings on the Hudson

select small

new age

in the guinea delete
pig back yard sneaking

out into
da woild

— Claire & the idea
mute of enclosure —
yr (meaning , Clare)
audio

bitching echo-depression

" without air we would ex - plode"

(roles
of " the soundz
thank
tank Hey!!) of there
u ,
jostling"
delete

press draw:
getting
to

this ploem [of water
needs
a many
kestrel floodlights
colors]

dumptrucks
& missions — re - eyeballed —
inside a thought balloon
the
treachery
butt the plastique of
we
boys want

to be air “delicate
”
deformation
in the early screen c
sun a
mooted r
(everyone’s). o
l
we’re leaving i
the guinea pigs n
here a

w
everybody’s Sir table r
non-nostalgic lost his e
vanishing the nasdaq n:
point city to a

bottle a
of
rocket h
snap shots
in media e
(anti)
loose
raisin c
gathering
hooking k
teeth !
back l
gotta
at this e
pay to not
hinge r
get
we
kicked
admit
back
from
out (never
post - postal
said
existence
a
the guinea pig peed
tree)
on these pants I'm now holding

titillating gerunds

mutually fund me

naturally counted on for an Ernst

duck

to make great clanging noises

as a bonus

whohaveyou

space is often

swiping
at one
like the
tentacles
of a
wind
machine
unquote

oblivious to

the proposal

of gaps

as proposals

But goodbyes
to alls
& thats

having a flower show

but why , hedge ?

as
if just
extracted

GET
TH
M

beauty's
critique
of
chance

Privacy Mutation Token

you hunt for the judge

who agrees

the reticent leveler off (too crowded & too empty)

the almost good

conducting a seminar

on coexistence

trope trophies

for the unearned

the un-urned?

(I'm feeling

somewhat

exposed writing

this in public

during a pandemic

& having just

read some Ed

Dorn rhymes

(the disambiguation

fairy don't

stop by

no more)

(but I *like*

being an adjunct)

& wishing he

was alive so

I could tell

him to fuck

off in a

friendly manner)

II.

In Boulder, CO
In 1980 the
kids in second
grade didn't like
me & said so
except Roberto
from Mexico who
invited me to count
water skimmers
& dig up worms. I'd
never seen a robin
til that spring. Why
were we there all
of a sudden in a
bigger apartment?
Dad was brought
to town as a
mediating presence
to help end the
Naropa Poetry Wars.
It was not a time
for reflection. I
went to the movies
by myself. 18 or 19
years later, listening
to Carl Rakosi read
& rap at the age of 95
I realized we were
in the gym of Lincoln
Elementary School &
some of us. Allen
proposed to Alice
at some point after
Ted died. God that
would have been
weird, if Mom had
said yes (thank you).
You are part of a
group whether you
like it or not, but
the name is always
wrong. Dorn liked
to golf. His & Jenny's
kids were older
& really nice to
me & Eddie that
twisted spring. Ro-
berto went by
Bobby by the way.
It was strange to be
being there—I
don't think my
brain was fully
formed, but my
internal voice
was more or less
in place in waves.
People in Boulder
had too much space
& not enough corner
school & looked up to
see Roberto say smiling
"I saw you scratch your
ass Anselm." My one
friend my age there.
Sentiment is such a
stupid pain. All I want
to know right now
is why Dick stopped
writing poems. Did he
really? Mom warned me
not everyone would
make it, in reference to
my excitement for me &
all my friends in SF in
1995. We mostly did
though, in that we write
still even through this
abject unhappiness the
planet gets to know
together & horribly
apart. I'm supposed to
get some scallions. The
19 year old writers don't
want to read pandemic
poems. I say I get it but
dig: everything written
now has the pandemic
in it, even if *it* don't
refer to *it*. Can't just

five year old Eddie
performing log rolls
for the non-community
of events called past was
suddenly superimposed
over Rakosi explaining
the usefulness of
cynicism: it keeps
you from being tricked!
(Guns N' Roses sucks)
Form of institutional
outlaw buddhist gent-
rification? Or more
like survival. We
survived the eighties

stores. The basic
kindness of certain
people became
apparent: Jack,
Jenny, Reed, Maia,
Kidd, Naomi, Kate
David, Dick, Bobby.
You know when
you sit on wooden
seats that make your
ass itch mercilessly?
I tried to secretly
scratch my ass in
class one day in that
really nice shitty

write your 9/11 poem
& think that's covered.
Course you did cover
it. I have no idea how
to live right now. But
I'm used to having no
ideas & being bad at
project-based applications.
I mean, I'm surprised I
even got this far, &
the floating heads
below are surprised
too. June & I are very
impressed by the 99 cent
pizza place on 2nd & A

because she likes the Sicilian slice

essentially a pizza slab

of great air injection & I like

their invention of a Chicken

Tikka Masala slice

which comes decorated

with elegant lines of purple

cabbage—they charge $4

for it though

from an ongoing untitled poem for Lewis Warsh

* * * *

I started writing to be myself, now
I start by imagining someone else
don't worry about pretending I'm not
trying to be you without finding myself
all over an advance on again's plateau
the writing is in the arrangement but
it (a pronoun) was never meant to begin
sleep on the couch & the monsters tower
walking single file away from destruction
monsters in dreams may know when to leave
sleep on the couch & wake up pantsless
in Berkeley at a party to celebrate your leaving
for work go straight awake to zoom to lie
and miss the conversation that made the reading
worth attending minor flashes of disgathering
light the year may attempt to deny its own end
but the year only began because a number said to
begin all us non-numbers want the year to end it
feels like the last non-digression ask they year
to choose between shoe or tree in a circle of years
and leave the speaker a mouth for a map
don't sweat the fruit fly that's been landing near
you all day it's been through its own non-year
hovering near the edge of the page prior

* * * *

The only opinion I could type was hostile dithering

Buses pass speaking silently: “masks required”

This barrier to my left, not the margin, which is also a barrier, may not appreciate my handwriting or general presence

Why would someone write something like that?

Well I’m not someone & I only write like when I’m grieving

Which is almost always, with intermittence, & inner mittens

Today’s conversation on bin laden was incredibly boring

But it’s 2020 & there are so many other agonistic layers to worklife

I want to read Phife Dawg’s mom’s memoir about Phife

Different day, different fruit fly on the other page

My brother has written a poem on all the times he’s moved

When I finish this page I’ll text him & tell him next to write a poem on all the times he’s been moved

& then work ethics were revealed to be an extreme series of overcompensations, though we knew that already but hadn’t said so aloud

The uninteresting pier building behind the colossal You Go Girl graffiti just turned bright blood red

Turning things around has a quiet crush on last chance

Everyone digs it when you admit to writing near strangers

He emptied many little transparent plastic bags into the east river, & slapped each one on the rail when he was done

Subways eating each other, aka passing, on the williamsburg bridge

You too may be eaten by someone simply passing by

Don't touch anything, don't breathe, don't be near

What appeared to be morning haze on eldridge was really smoke from the west coast fires

The coasts took turns absorbing punishment this year

Like Dan Quisenberry we find deliveries in our flaws

* * * *

To withhold with
total intimacy, to flirt only with
estrangement, to wonder secretly
into a microphone, three seconds
of rain, three smears of raindrops
I see you in leather in stories on
a phone, the reveal makes every
thing boring, no things but in
events, the sum of all
my trinkets, I want this
to be something else
so I can show it off before
burying it, I want to churn
butter onstage, well

maybe not, maybe that's
too much setup, I want
one more conversation with Lewis
an actual goodbye with Ted G.
another word with Bill, who made
taking anyone seriously feel
like the elegant thing to do

* * * *

Yup, I mean up too late again—I wonder
what it would be like to be a punchline
machine. No, I wonder what a punchline
machine feels, no like. I hate like. That's
my new position: to hate like. Like is
no longer an intermediary I'm willing to
accept. Not that like cares. I clearly care
too much, & this has always been a
problem for me, though I try not to let
people know I care too much, & that
has also become a problem. If you used
to love me but you replaced me in your
heart with Jesus, I'm cool with that.
You could even say I'm relieved, though
you might find it strange to say that yourself.
I have loved so many people secretly
I wonder if I'm not on trial somewhere
in an empty court room. If you've ever
suspected I love you, I hereby give you
permission to validate your suspicion.
Unless you think it won't help. We

may have to discuss what help means.
But we may also never get to speak in
person again, & defining or redefining help
between us is a conversation I can only
have in person. In person is a strange phrase
too. I haven't felt in person for a long time
but apparently being in person means someone
else is there too. I think that's wrong
but who cares what I think. Now
I'm stuck between is there & who
cares. Our pronoun-based phrases are
wildly inaccurate for all situations. I
wish they had been more available when I was
a kid. Less and less obviously it all shakes
down to the mesh, an awkwardly amused
pathos conjoined to a failing ability not
to notice the house band made of special
guests from the secret police posing as
marathon champs from the mid-80s. Even
my mother thought that was Grete Waitz
living across the street. At the fake pond
our reading was disrupted by Ezekiel:
33 blasting from sudden speakers
dragged to ducks by the Sunday millers.
The swans were the first to swim away.
We read Lewis poems a little closer to
the road, to be sermonized only faintly
if at all under lines from Alien Abduction.
The same person who said no one gives
him gifts followed by saying it's the
thought that counts, reminding us of the
simultaneous keeling over of at least
two No Standing signs the other day.

This reminds me of Adam developing
a crush on photographs of Patsy Southgate
in 1996 & wondering if she was still
available even if fifty years older than
him & all the way back east. Your
friend needs to be able to ask their own
questions. M was wearing pants a four-
legged person could have fit into, but
we wouldn't put it that way out loud.
Dinosaur-era bird with scythe-like
beak sheds light, like me, on avian
diversity. Shoe, or tree?

* * * *

& now every
one's icebergs are just a little more
skewed

the reports
from the alternate
sites are definitively
skewed

I'm also that former mayor
leaking hp sauce
from the glare

& the pressure
of trying to talk reality
into flipping

itself over

if they can make it

it's not art

navigating this odd off
season

is there room
in the parthenon

your pineapple

signals

from?

* * * *

the margin's another look out
on the threshold of prickly thighs

three bites of a three dollar sandwich
justification's back booby prize

for aesthetic loitering versus

we likes what we knows
to be uselesses in boths

white and milk
chocolate chip pancakes

or in privacies
steeped in ordinary
slips of experience

I'll have mutability
without a loop
next time anyone (they
won't) asks

* * * *

after all the student debt's erased
we need a massive squad
of non–federally trained
therapists to flow through
the mean driveways
of the country

& vice versatility
every owl visible
is an active doppel
ganger "mosquitoes
learn not to mess
with you when you
swat them"
—popular science

once I bit
a sandwich
in the face

corner hurt

hurts

* * * *

every sentence
horrifying & even

immunity
to declaratives
could function
as a kindness
of advice

(*we only reject your certainty*)

A fake house

a blue facade

I ate half

the fake sandwich

Sudden flash of
seeing Lewis at the
14th st. Y swimming pool 1984
we went there for
a year or two
after Ted died & Alice
looked around
for things
we could do
(trust?)

order as you will

* * * *

November 30 & I'm wondering
if curiosity, in me, can win out
over despair, at least for a while
longer. I like the looseness of a

while. When despair approaches
I get even, but low-level feel
for the self-destruct button.
Which turns out to be another
um-bilical hernia. Doctor Hof-
stetter playing wack a hole with
my belly the size of which is hard
to gauze (I prefer loose clothing).
One anti-despair image I retain
having invented it just now is
wearing an oversized flannel
shirt at the age of sixty-five.
When I'm helpful I'm surprised.
When I'm grateful I burst into
tears. I'm told I don't talk about
my feelings enough, but I know
on the inside how self-absorbed
I am, & the poets lets it flow
with buzzing fracked apology
incisions (Nesh vomiting foam)
the live ear has no room not to
take, this poem may be inter-
upted by cat surgery soon, R.
Smithson was just a baby when
he died you don't know, Piper
digs Empson enough to let me
what, distract myself in theory
by planning a tribute, do *you*
really need *more* of my feel-
ings? Emphasis takes care of
yeah she has that option. An
aside that concludes things.
Leniency deserving no norms.

* * * *

if anyone has any spare time & would like to help fold, staple, & mutilate, please let us know

it is rare when a real writer becomes also a real restaurateur

& form is all beautiful & typical & unread & self-destructive in complete & enjoyable fashion

admired by a giant who likes them

and yet, dude, the soundtrack did not invent silence

or, baby, maybe it did did do that that

it's when you sprinkle a little ground conspiracy on the proceedings

write a poem called "impractical advice" that begins "lay back in relation to certain people" we texted ourselves recently

make a map of z one & done

some people support disagreement in principle without realizing it

some of those people like to hang out after readings

the places that still let you hang out afterward are where you'll find them

I saw no hands during the zoom meeting but knew they were all wringing

hoody production meets obstinate website

we screamed 57 times in five and a half minutes

hard not to talk about that at the critique

placing bonus succulent has proved elusive

to be elusive vs I forgot about possibility

between pages only one page may prove attainable or retainable

depending on our sense of what tainable might mean

disAnselmed disanselmed

the practice test validated repetition

when we took the title IX course five years later all the situations were unchanged

we felt awful that the bullied office worker was still crying tears of frustration in his car, & that his bullying co-worker remained oblivious and at large

completing the online course at multiple institutions was no consolation

one of those institutions may be taking transformation seriously, according to minutes

handed the old language as template for new situations

we're all (interrupted)

& yet when therapy points to our powerlessness we gap

we gasp?

we gap

we don't want power, we have too much on the inside, the interior, the temporary source

uninterested in outlasting

now decide where surface & source meet

end the night with pop songs & other songs

end the night

it's only 5:59pm & we have to make dinner so but to the last thoughtless

can't pick up presents when the untouch is in command

everyone can reply

* * * *

They tell you what they're doing in order to steer you into submission

They look perennially for the incompetent replacement

The dominant incompetent administers anger elliptically

Waking up begins to feel unsafe

* * * *

Your footnotes lack persona—a foot rub might help

Children's Dresses, Boys' Suits, Underwear, 2A Bar, Novelties

They overdosed on failing better after mail broke the demagogue

* * * *

The conversation between gratitude & irony is where realism goes to listen

He's offended only when the phone rings

The poems become photographs to avoid publication

* * * *

This month you're averaging fewer steps each day than you did last month

You're averaging fewer steps a day this year than last year

The pandemic has reduced your daily steps by 2,500 on average at least this year

You're clearly not pacing enough at home

It's hard to pace in a small apartment

Pacing often requires privacy

Privacy is not your friend anymore

* * * *

Sometimes I prefer to re-order dinner

Reaching the past I mean part of the day where amusement replaces despair—it helps to have the sun go down & the light freak out

A proxy of determination in a cosmic discharge salon

We said that eras ago

* * * *

We've ordered different elements of medical

* * * *

A few days later a refusal of pickled asparagus under a cheap heater

The problem with the continuous present: you keep getting put back together

Tap to zoom

* * * *

I'd prefer being chaste by a bear

Or chatted up somewhere narrow minus eye contact

Dude dying in Dakota denies cause

Don't remember to forget on purpose (motto of the exhumed whores & poets guild)

We just got our first seven stars from Himalayan Vision

* * * *

Brandon loved an image

Jess liked "Good luck!"

Paolo liked "I signed it the other night"

Pippa liked "Hi Pippa, June is out with Astrid right now at the park"

* * * *

evoluntary?

evoluntarily

like us you get things done only when you're supposed to do something else

* * * *

plaid ass

& the unrecognizable country

"

rejuvenate
the

disrejuvenated

. . ."

Selected Resurrections

the words get together
in the early morning
& decide on who they're
gonna fail that day

they <u>pick</u> people
the people who will
go on to say " language
failed me today "

*****

Vermeer was something of a visitor
Ecumenical (look up) & withheld.
Are they far enough apart outside ?
I travelled through barelife to find
her dream was really in my backyard.
So real life must be happening elsewhere.
In the cushion on fire where you sit
Moving in pictures on the phone sliding
In on two-dollar bills wearing the
Sudden address you barely refuse.
To ground pork we're all loose teeth
Positing entertainment as oblivious
Standard. What, you don't talk to
Collected bits of meat? I put gray
Around my brain to let it breathe
I was told by age in an interview.
A vital sort of non-profession &
A refusal to intersect with the
Crossed-out heads peppering white
Space just write. They are false
Starts & nonetheless records of
Hopeful betrayal. Key lime ginger
Almonds hurt hurtling up rose
Hills in search of survivors. We
Seem behind screen to have
Reduced alienation to a series
Of gaffes. Phooey strikes back
Gloriously far-flung from
The point. Disguised locations.
Say what's there. Confined

To bed each utterance commands.
It's all this ill-fitting conglomerate
in the incomplete happenstance
something constantly expanding
sideways in the past, free as
hell from present definition.

for BB & BG

on all my substitute birthdays

O syrup of mammoths !

O the charities !

oh plankton !

“ oh thank you ”

oh Tartars , and how many

of our loves have you illuminated with

your heart your breath

O the Polish summers ! those drafts !

those black and white teeth !

oh fertility ! beloved of the Western world

oh mothers you will have made the little tykes

oh god its wonderful

O sole mio, hot diggety, nix, “ I wather think I can ”

oh hôtel, you should be merely a bed

“Oh Sun , I’m so grateful to you!”

“ oh you know why ”

“ plunging and exuding from

the distended grin of its loved one’s O,”

“ Oh. ”

O for a long sound sleep and so forget it! ”

O my enormous piano, you are not like being outdoors

Oh pure blue of a footstep, have you stolen

March?

Turn, oh turn!

            Oh my palace of oranges,

junk shop, staples, ember, basalt;

I'm a child again when I was really

miserable, a grope pizzicato

O black looks at the base of the spine!

O paradise!

O pain!

O perfect obstruction on track."

O hobble and kobble Dolores

oh Basket Weavers' Conference!

o Sylvette!

"Oh Leaves of Grass!

"O fat-assed configurations

          and volutions   of ribbed sand which the sea

never reaches!"

O panic of drying mushrooms!

" o toe ! "   Oh Bismarck!

forgiving you not, for I am weeping from a tall wet dream, oh.

o Gladstone !

“ Ô reine Überschreigung !”

“ Oh the droppings from the trees ! the little clam shells,

their bosoms thrust into the clouds and kiss-stained! ”

Oh aspirations prancing like an elephant in a skirmish !

O coupling of strangers in the longings of grease !

O cufflinks of danger in the lozenge of geese !

O doubtful verifiers of the quality of cerise-streaked pus

O comatose lips of charcoal going down oh the horizon!

O comarose hips of charbroiled going clowning horizons!

O great soulful scandal in the courtyard of clairvoyance !

O loud timber leg of ore listening to the abutting hoots

& the compensatory descriptions of tin in the banks !

oh my dear oh “La Ronde,” erase what is assured & ours

oh leap !

Oh say can you see Alma

of heart so sick

O boy, their childhood was like so many oatmeal cookies.

O fateful eagerness !

O the amusing audience to all words shivers

O sins of sex and kisses of birds at the end of the penis

O the bread of colleens butters the rain.

O the glassy towns are fucked by yaks.

Oh be not silent on this distressing holiday whose week

has been a chute of sand down which no factories or castles tumbled:

O forest, o brook of spice, o cool gaze of strangers !

O infinite our siestas !

"O friends of my heart ! "

Oh Jane, is there no more frontier ?

o sweet Roman light

in ribbons over the prairie's collapse !

Oh be droll, be jolly

and be temperate !

O my darling sculpture garden,

you are sorry I went to Alaska ?

O sweet neurosis of a May jump!

Oh what is this light that holds us fast?

Oh! my heart, although it zounds better in French

Oh yes.

Oh Mackie's knife has a fake handle so it can

express its meaning as well as his.

O Boris Pasternak , it may be silly

Oh fie ! for shame !

Oh! kangaroos, sequins, chocolate sodas !

" Suis-je belle, ô nausée?"

or greener than now if you were with me O you

Consumer Affairs Unenclosed Sidewalk Café License

an example of a trouvaille
is the finding of a biblical
artifact, but I like to write
memoirs for other people
that was a lie, why would
I want to burst forth from
your memories, it is hard
enough to hold here, the
bills continue to change
shape, voices reduced to
type surge forward near
but never really within
the person I bear from
hour to hour, words living
to disappear get everything
just wrong enough, I see
you've altered your appearance
in the recent past, let us
muffle in specific proximity
or be muffled, in training of
some kind—the training
this wakefulness requires
outside of the grouper I
often pitch administration to
the fish, it's my bejeweled
sacrifice, a kind of refund
of the second person, I mean
refusal, or a typo of, the re-
enactment of turning to, will
I know you'll wander enough

to ask wonder to stay hidden
to to to be called upon
when play is bound up with
future possession, railing
soulfully draws a perimeter
or a perrymeter, on call
our inflexible lack of horse
riding experience informs
the troubadour academy
with the desire of chimp
city, to make feel blithe
blithe's monsturd daddy
this card describes you
scam likely is calling again
one thing scam's got a
good grip on is remorse
wanting life in scam's
composition to stimulate
my life moments, or not
speaking as a functional
menace beneath the
library wallpaper on the
armory walls withing
which hyenas scout the
migration between bouts
of coupling—did you
survive, accurately, your
last attempt at coupling
with your nearby hyena?
you've been nominated to
apply, as far as we go,
freedom from suffering
is only necessary for

freedom offromoffrom
the grass lozenge really
enjoyed it when the
wind lozenge blew
through the drops are
insular was the next
thing said last week I
taught in person mask
on, performed litany
with audience mask on
attended Judah & Ava's
b'nai mitzvah mask on—
I'm totally a functional
menace, I guess? I guess
How many types of surface
does our imagination
require? As many wads
of ones your field can
hold, to see and unsteel
in a disturbance, stalk-
like reflictions, apropot
to anything

Self-involved poem for Brandon B. on his Bday

I wonder about the quiet
students—don't we all?
In that generation gap
I explerience within for
Myself, I am the perpetual
Blank of a present student
Self, slowly making aware-
ness come to bleed (I ain't
got time to bleedeth
inherent tears of ass-ertion
going laterally forward)
its disdain for labels in
anarchy class: cancel or
delete? In the case of Afghan
Whigs its like I located
some timing of the funky
so what vein, & then D
told me he was always
doubtful on Dulli, so
maybe my slobject is to
rehear all of 1993—I
left a doppelgangrene there
Today in zooms of our lives
everyone froze except me
not long after no one could
hear me. It was a lot like 1987
& being 15. I wondered (pigeon
just landed behind me, orange-eyeing
my setup) if it wasn't
time for the post-ghost
to appear in countertime.
I'm still wondering. Had an
all expression in eyelines
conversation in person today.
It was this rare bird thing.
an absolute admission of love
by the last book stand in
Manhattan. Presence is the
Establishment of listening's
Practice. Gotta think about
That. Even if you only think
In the gnarly future
Future's end makes way for.
As a quiet student learning
How to learn all the time
I hate what teaching does to
Me & my personal irony.
Soon, which is a money
Problem, I will never let
Anyone put me in charge
in charge of again.

Poem written during a zoom meeting

The   doorbus   ringeth

multiply

everyone dies

extra slowly

Poem written just before turning fifty

Mickey Mantle didn't believe he'd
make it to fifty, a book told me.

David told me it was forty
actually. The Babe only just

made it past fifty. "The termites
have got me," Babe told Connie.

Dad, Steve Carey, Albert Notley
Jr.: none of them made fifty. Bill

Russell just left at 88. Beulah
was mad she wouldn't make 100

when cancer came her way at 94
I dreamt, when she was in hip

replacement surgery in 2011
the doc put a little red white &

blue ABA basketball in there, to
keep it all together. Is Claudell

Washington really gone, Rickey?
I'll never be older than Phil Niekro

I'll always be older than Juan Soto
Come home Brittney Griner—be

let go & brought home. Where's
that goddamned bridge? Il Punto!?

They say the Bostonians say Bucky
Fucking Dent (a sentence! a poem!)

but Judy our neighbor who dated
Adam the rocker whispered "Fucky

Dent" to me once in the old daze
Teddy Higuera & Larry Gura

Tippy Martinez & Scott McGregor
Yankee killers all—but George Brett

was a fucking Balrog, a demon
from the ancient world. Actually

no—he was Morgoth—the dark lord
Edgar Martínez was the fucking Balrog

*****

You can't keep yourself in sync

It's old non-news

But agency! says

Wrong detour

Slap jingle helicopter buzz

We meet the mighty lost

Who were frail in presentation

Always so

To form the copy & banish its essence

Now the chair bites up

Were aims finally substitutes for arms?

One, being a fraction, given time

Has to reverse the deep dive

Don't be angry forever

Only on the inside

* * * * * * * *

Under that predrawn surface

Some kind of decision feigns

Getting made

I miss the come on

Getting made feigns

While all this madeness

Bends out

Correct that space

Add on in turns

Call night an unending sound

Of eternity's anguish

*****

when we speak

of ourselves
interchangeably
and
in
conclusion

a budget is just
a snapshot

a painter with day job
as accountant
informed me

Freegrets

couple no shirts, fear of shoes, tell it what it is
avatari: I too make spiral tracks on the seafloor
when K wants more courage she looks at the way
Rose draws a leg, the barn your studio, one leg
ghosted, one hip impinged and set for replace-
ment, Mera from Xebel, Jackson Hyde, & Arthur
Curry, constellated, half a melon holding up the shack
by which mammal shadows repose, the mutineer
may be saved by the buoyancy of citrus, the living room
corner my dusky shark deskolalia, the mutineer
doesn't want to be there for one more lunch, chilling
though, chilling like a villain I trained the 3-yr-old
to tell the babysitter poet, when I want more courage
I call courage's agent, no, I make myself pick a place
in page space to start, imagine if we'd had different
teachers, in paint in person, who said do life drawing
overwhelmed by red water surfaces, from a real horse?
your imagination reinvents red from memory every
time you hear the word red, reds added to seeing
have their say, they ran from the waves but stayed
in the painting, reflection digging the purple light
& spurning reflectivity, there's a large out of focus
reflectivity monster roaming the seaside, formally
and emotionally she felt the need for lifeguards
as plasma in tights I make occasional comments
on havoc, mutiny's inner edges in the plane, will
they prevent the sea worms from eating the casual
cop, if not simply tubular shapes alight in the four
ground, are they bobbit worms or bristle worms
pyrosomes or sea squirts, because of the lack of hard

evidence the Mongolian death worm is widely accepted
as just being a legend, don't talk about money, don't
talk about being sick, don't talk about yourself, dude
looks facelessly relaxed for a mutiny, realism is a
variable, or is it a variability—go ask Alex, making lists
predates all so-called generations, the way universality
ignores aliens, but I need to borrow money, getting sick
gets me out of things, & I can't assert myself anywhere
but here, yellow sinews playing with scale, inflation—
whatever, fax me when stag-flation looms in the doom-
light, too many drunk Santas fucking with my red, mother
magenta, what did the mutineer do to the clouds?

for/after Katherine Bradford

Corner Eye

I too might inspect
the corner of the carpet
if I knew I could stash
golden paperclips and
random puzzle pieces
between its surface &
whatever that other
shit below it is. Hi. I
disagree with the writer
who said on the comic
book resources website
that the ability to fly by
screaming really, really
loud is inherently silly.
I just typed something
really dumb, but I came
back to make sure I
copped to doing so. A
recent claims number
is 19031582. Don't
usually type poems
on the computer. Just
crossed out five lines
about my health, or
actually about my
dislike of occupying
medical habitats in
the civic spheres.
I asked a hip specialist
how much it would hurt

right after getting a hip
replacement. It's really
tempting to break out
of the costume in that
kind of extended
temporary moment.
He said it will feel
like being kicked in
the hip by a donkey
but the donkey will
get smaller every day.
You have a pretty
good idea how hard
it is to go on from
here. I'm going to
start teaching again
the day after tomorrow.
I have to preserve
tomorrow as the day
I get ready for teaching.
The main thing to do
is wake up and not
trick yourself out of
having a mind. Or, to
give your mind a wide
berth in order to function.
That may be a way
of recognizing mind
actually. I don't know.
I have subscribed to
no philosophies. No
philosophy has my
credit card number.

No autopay. I know
how this sounds.
Don't worry. The
distortion is coming.
Some kind of slash
through. Camo in
public. I defended
snakes on twitter
right before writing
everything after
the first dozen lines.
I hate the relentless
way this won't go
anywhere but down.
But by saying so
I become available
to shedding hate.
I'm having weird
memory gaps. For
me. I'm saying this
both on and below
this surface. I'm
sorry if I don't always
remember your
name. The dumb
thing said isn't in
the poem.

Still Here

Is it weird for marks
to be named mark
when someone says
we mark the occasion?
When you're named
anselm this isn't something
you think about
even if I am thinking
about it now, if this is
thinking. My apologies.
I was going to start
this In My Mind
by typing "I am reverting
but I don't know
in what direction."
Reverting in this instance
may mean thinking about
dying. Not what you want.
But I can't help the way
this is going. I don't think
you can really prepare
for missing someone.
And then you can.
And then you can't.
And then that absence
in order to be itself
is always something else.

for Paul & Sarah

To Cedar

Lake Garda's winds blow the chips
out of their bowls another common
distortion, MAG
in big white letters across
a burgundy drape hanging from

a castle window in the old fortress
transitioning
into local museum

Aperol through
a straw goes down too fast, breaking
squibbles in the shanks
of giants, purple
pastrami layers of mountains
change colors
by the minute, looming
as feint. In Padua
the heat is near to Needles
little lizards
reimagining the gulley
outside Giotto's starscape
so oddly figured as realist
by the intro video
an irreality tv version
of wall text. I swooned

for all my anti-
redemptive tendencies
at the site
of Jericho's sleep

goats and an angel making
a perimeter in a high arching square
of another desert

Folds of robes in the sunflats, bugging

Rearrangement requires bone fragments
if not the whole hoary skeletux

Easy to get the first drink here
the cove more brood than bruise

You are in the hospital after a stroke
& you will see me soon in New York

This feels impossible
to cut up

I can only be late everywhere in
your honor, a continuation honor burns
in envy to keep up with

The second drink
suitably stronger
finally arrives
delivered by coot & crested grebe

Does war dream of war
Onoda asks
in the jungle
of Werner's twilight?

Poem Inspired by Everything

I would just like to point out, but I always end
up pointing in. "Everyone's holier than thou! &
I'm definitely rolling the dice!" a camo-clad
gent w/ dork beer a good sixteen fiats away
exclaims—just as I was measuring how to use
inkling in a work: this report brought to you by
the Tompkins Square Park Skocial Mistancing
Fretwork, & Aaron Shurin's elegant purple mask
on instagram matching a doubled pair of purple
gloves I cycled by on B a minute ago—they did
possess hands, attached to gaily striding arms
accompanied by too-comfortable (a projection)
smiles. My own powdered transparent gloves
make my fingers look desiccated—a thought
parallel to a fuzzy pink gasmask sported by
a fellow strolling by twenty feet away, fifty
masks for seventy bucks at the stationary
store on A, if you ask, grayish blue and intent
a whole other present, my idea of a sentence:
a summary of daily briefings delivered by
rainbow buntings, the horseshoe bar selling
drinks to go to a politely spaced line, & when
the drawn, I mean dawn, distracted from its
game of catch with figure & ground, speaks
I just keep listening to this fish, aghast at
the split fins I and we call legs. I hear sitting
in these fins, sunlight a costume of horizontal
neon bars, early pandemic bloom lines coming
through cracks the clouds briefly perform

for Charles North

Don’t Forget

Notes

"In Betweener" is dedicated in memoriam to John Ashbery.

"Proof ('everything you are gone slightly mad . . .')" was written to be performed for apexart's Double Take series curated by Albert Mobilio and Jen Firestone. We were given the word *proof* to consider without any other constraint. I decided to start by listing things I knew to be true but couldn't necessarily prove, beginning with the last time I saw my father in person.

"Theories of Influence" is composed of sentences from W. G. Sebald's prose narrative *The Rings of Saturn* (translated by Michael Hulse). Like Bigfoot, Sebald's narrator in that particular book is always blurry, if only when risking being seen.

"Press Conference" happened because John Yau writes pantoums as warm-ups, and Marshawn Lynch, the great Seattle Seahawks running back, gave press conferences in which he'd say one thing over and over to every question.

Any poem herein that starts with a set of asterisks is its own poem. They could have all been in the Big Sketchbook Semi-Survival Poems section, but balance demanded spreading them out. Those poems and all the poems in the Big Sketchbook section were written by hand during 2020, and the variations in type size, the deliberate misspellings, the non-chronology, and the wrecked inner commentary are part of what they are on the page. I just wanted to get the typed versions as close as possible to the handwritten versions.

"Wobble Factory" was written across 2019 and originally published by Absolute Slab Editions (an imprint I invented just for this poem—I'll send it to you if you write me at anselmberrigan@aol.com—it has a great cover). It was circulated free as a pdf to anyone who asked. My thanks to the many people who responded via email to tell me things about it, and the many bardsters who said things that got blended into the work.

John Coletti Imitation Racket tells it what it is. I don't know if section titles in a book of poems need italics or quotation marks.

"Last Thrift" is a complete line-by-line ripoff of Ron Padgett's poem "First Drift," if one informed by my honorary status as member of the nyc chapter of the cockroach/feline underground network.

The poem beginning either with "don't worry / it's self-guiding" and/or "(get your ass / to mars)" is dedicated to Andrei Codrescu—this book is also secretly dedicated to Andrei, who took me to Romania in 2015 and changed my life. I should mention that "Breathlahem" is the title of a semi-secret Jim Brodey work.

"Privacy Mutation Token" is dedicated to Anne Waldman, June Berrigan, and Bobby from Boulder, wherever he may be.

The BB and BG in the poem beginning with the line "Vermeer was something of a visitor . . ." are Bill Berkson and Bob Glück, and was written out of reading a conversation between them that appeared in *The Brooklyn Rail.* Bill is also the Bill mentioned in the poem for Lewis Warsh, "… who made / taking anyone seriously feel / like the elegant thing to do …" I don't think it's necessary to reveal names and sources much of the time, but I've been fortunate to have many good friends who are no longer present, and don't want to miss the chance to miss them out loud a little more particularly this time around.

"on all my substitute birthdays" has got to be the most obvious thing I've ever done, and I hope it shows.

"Poem written just before turning fifty" was written when David Kirschenbaum asked whether I had anything for a baseball-themed issue of *Boog City*. Thank you, David—and that one's for you and Jim and my dad.

"Freegrets" came out of being asked by Tyhe Cooper to respond to an artwork in *The Brooklyn Rail* Rail Curatorial Projects 2022 show *Singing in Unison*. This big beautiful seriously red Katherine Bradford painting was part of the show, and so I wrote something out of what looking at the painting, which is called *Mutiny*, was doing to me, or what I thought it was doing to me.

The Everything in "Poem Inspired by Everything" comes from Charles North's book *Everything and Other Poems*. That book, along with Claire Hong's *Upend* (which was published under her former name, Claire Meuschke), were lifelines for me in the plain sense of making me want to write amidst all the pain. I hope this note makes both Charles and Claire blush.

How does anyone know when to stop writing notes?

Acknowledgments

I could thank tons of people here, but for specific feedback, inspiration, counsel, and support for this particular and hopefully elegant mess I want to thank Karen Weiser, Sylvie Berrigan, June Berrigan, Courtney Bush, John Yau, John Coletti, Hoa Nguyen, Dale Smith, Simone White, Claire Hong, CAConrad, Peter Gizzi, Alice Notley, Edmund Berrigan, erica kaufman, Carolyn Ferrucci, Tyhe Cooper, Matt Longabucco, Mónica de la Torre, Jonathan Allen, Zach Wollard, Marley Freeman, Phong Bui, LaTasha Diggs, Patricia Spears Jones, Jen Firestone, Jen Fisher, Simon Pettet, Kyle Dacuyan, Halsey Rodman, Alexandro Segade, Don Share, Elinor Nauen, Marcella Durand, Rich O'Russa, John Godfrey, Charles North, Nick Sturm, Joshua Beckman, Edwin Torres, Eileen Tabios, Paolo Javier, Jeanne Liotta, Cedar Sigo, Eric Baus, Roberto Tejada, Ann Lauterbach, and Ron Padgett.

Shout out to Club Confetti for being the late night lockdown ground and sounding board a lot of these poems needed.

Versions of some of these poems have been published in the following mags, journals, anthologies, and otherwise clandestine publications:

AMIN, The Arts Fuse, As of Late, Boog City, The Brooklyn Rail, Castle Grayskull, Critical Quarterly, Elderly, Hurricane Review, Jaking It, Journal, Luigi Ten Co, Marsh Hawk Review, NYC From the Inside: NYC through the Eyes of the Poets Who Live Here, Poetry, Poets on Death, the tiny, Touch the Donkey, TYPO, and *Works and Days.*

My thanks to all the folks working on these endeavors, for inviting me to take part, and for keeping the poems in sight.